→HOW LONG DOES IT TAKE TO MAKE A FOSSIL?

BY EMILY HUDD

CONTENT CONSULTANT
Alison Olcott, Associate Professor,
Department of Geology, University
of Kansas

CAPSTONE PRESS
a capstone imprint

Fact Finders Books are published by Capstone Press,
1710 Roe Crest Drive, North Mankato, Minnesota 56003
www.mycapstone.com

Library of Congress Cataloging-in-Publication Data
Names: Hudd, Emily, author.
Title: How long does it take to make a fossil? / by Emily Hudd.
Description: North Mankato, Minnesota : Capstone Press, [2020] | Series: How
   long does it take? | Audience: Grades 4 to 6. | Includes bibliographical
   references and index.
Identifiers: LCCN 2018058406 (print) | LCCN 2018060462 (ebook) | ISBN
   9781543572988 (ebook) | ISBN 9781543572926 (hardcover) | ISBN 9781543575392 (pbk.)
Subjects: LCSH: Fossilization--Juvenile literature. | Fossils--Juvenile literature.
Classification: LCC QE721.2.F6 (ebook) | LCC QE721.2.F6 H83 2020 (print) |
   DDC 560/.41--dc23
LC record available at https://lccn.loc.gov/2018058406

All internet sites appearing in back matter were available and accurate when this book was sent to press.

Editorial Credits
Editor: Marie Pearson
Designer and production specialist: Dan Peluso

Photo Credits
AP Images: Felipe Dana, 8; iStockphoto: aristotoo, cover (bottom), Blackbeck, cover (top),
Extreme-Photographer, 14–15; Science Source: David Davis, 24, Phil Degginger, 28, Stephen J. Krasemann,
20; Shutterstock Images: BGSmith, 17, Breck P. Kent, 23, Nuntiya, 19, stihii, 27, thoron, 12–13, tropicdreams,
6–7, W. Scott McGill, 5, wong yu liang, 10

Design Elements: Red Line Editorial

TABLE OF CONTENTS

FINDING FOSSILS

A class is on a field trip at a state park. They hike on a dusty trail. They pick up many rocks and sticks. One student finds a unique rock. It has swirly lines on one side. The lines are indented.

FACT Some fossils show plants and animals that lived millions of years ago!

She puts her finger in one of the grooves. She traces it to the edge of the rock. The swirly lines look like the shell of a snail. She has found a fossil!

A fossil is a rock with the preserved **remains** and traces of plants and animals on it. It can also show animal activities such as footprints.

Animal footprints and dinosaur bones make large fossils. Museums display some dinosaur fossils. Some people collect fossils.

Fossils tell people about the history of life on Earth. **Paleontologists** study them. They can learn what animals and plants were alive in the past and where they lived. It takes thousands of years to make a fossil!

Ammonites were ancient sea creatures whose fossils look like large snail shells.

paleontologist—a person who studies fossils and is an expert on them

CHAPTER ONE

GETTING BURIED

There are several events that must happen for a fossil to form. First, there must be living plants and animals. They walk on land. They swim in the ocean. They grow from the earth. Some live for many years. Some live for only a few days. Second, an animal or plant must die. The third step is that the animal or plant needs to be protected from rotting away. It needs protection from **oxygen** and bacteria. Oxygen and bacteria break down dead animals and plants. They cause the remains to disappear before making a fossil.

oxygen—a gas that is used for many things on Earth, including breathing and breaking things down

Many kinds of animals can fossilize after they die, including sea turtles.

Mudslides can quickly cover the remains of many living things.

Protection from rotting often happens when the animal or plant is buried. Gravel and sand are common **sediments**. Many dead animals and plants get covered by gravel and sand. But these coverings are not likely to make fossils. The grains

in those coverings are too big. A sediment with smaller grains is needed. Mud is a better covering. It is thick. It slows down oxygen and bacteria trying to pass through it.

sediment—material such as small grains of sand, rock, or earth matter that are moved by wind or water before they settle

scientist—a person who uses observation and experiments to study the natural world

Left exposed to the wind and sun, even hard bones will crumble away before they can fossilize.

No matter the material, the dead animal or plant needs to be fully covered. Most fossils do not form on open land. Remains on open land are exposed to many things that cause bodies to break down. Wind and rain break things apart. Animals may crush or feed on the remains.

NEARLY COMPLETE

One of the most complete Tyrannosaurus rex fossils was found in 1990. Scientists found more than 90 percent of its bones. It is on display at the Field Museum in Chicago, Illinois.

Sometimes only a portion of animal or plant remains is buried. For example, the head might be buried, and the body is not. The head turns into a fossil. The body **decomposes**. Large animals can be buried in multiple places. So bones from one dinosaur could end up on different rocks. Some bones might make a fossil. Some bones might not.

For many reasons, most fossils are not perfect. Too much water could wipe out all the materials. Or the parts could decompose too quickly. Fossils are buried for millions of years before they are found.

decompose—to break down into smaller pieces

CHAPTER TWO

LAYERS AND LAYERS

Fossils are made slowly over time. It takes many layers of sediment. The first layer is the ground the dead animal or plant falls on. The second layer of a fossil is the protective covering. Then, the third layer of sediment and many more add up over time. This is the longest part of making a fossil. It happens very slowly. Rocks, sand, mud, and other materials pile up for thousands of years.

FACT

Strata is a word for layers of rocks.

It takes a long time for layers of rock to form.

Layers add up differently depending on the environment. On land, **gravity** helps layers form. Dirt, rocks, and mud build up. Sometimes wind or water currents can slow down layer formation. Wind and sea currents can move top layers. Animals can walk on and move layers.

gravity—a force that pulls objects with mass together; gravity pulls objects down toward the center of Earth

Water is constantly moving sand on the seafloor.

The remains get buried deeper and deeper. The weight of many layers creates pressure. Pressure helps form fossils. The sand, mud, and gravel get packed together. Air and water are pressed out.

Sedimentary rocks form separately from fossils, but many fossils are found in them. This is because the way sedimentary rocks form is ideal for fossils. Loose sediment forms layers. The layers build up over time. They get packed together to become rock. Sedimentary rocks are made of **minerals**, pieces of clay, other rocks, grains of sand, and gravel. They cover 75 percent of Earth's surface. Remains of animals and plants in many places can fall on them. As layers pile up, animal remains can get trapped in them.

FACT
There are many kinds of sedimentary rock. Gravel can form into a type called conglomerate. Sand becomes sandstone. Mud becomes shale.

mineral—a material found in nature that is not an animal or plant

Many fossils have been found in sedimentary rocks.

Like fossils, sedimentary rocks take many years to form. **Geologists** estimate that it takes thousands of years to make 0.04 inches (1 millimeter) of sedimentary rock. The rocks that most fossils are found in can contain preserved remains from different time periods. Some animals or plants might have lived at the beginning of the 1,000 years. Others might have lived at the end of that time.

geologist—a person who studies rocks and is an expert on them

CHAPTER THREE

FOSSILIZATION

Scientists think it takes 10,000 years or more for fossils to form. Since they form underground, it is hard to study just how long it takes. A fossil can be made in different ways under the pressure of many layers of sediment. Compression is one type of **fossilization**. It makes two-dimensional fossils. This means it is flat. Sediment covers a leaf. When the sediment presses the leaf at high pressure, the leaf decomposes. It leaves behind coal. The coal leaves a dark mark on the sediment.

fossilization—the process of dead animal or plant remains turning into rocks

SOFT PARTS

Soft things such as skin, organs, or flower petals break down easily. Soft parts of plants generally break down in a few weeks or months. Soft parts of animals decompose in a few months or years. This means animals and plants made mainly of soft parts do not usually turn into fossils.

Eventually, the sediment hardens into rock. The dark marks of the preserved remains are inside the rock. The fossil is found if the rock splits. The marks can be seen on both sides of the rock.

When leaves fossilize, they typically form compression fossils.

Another way a fossil can be made is by replacement. This means another material takes the place of the original parts of the animal or plant before they decompose. Typically, soft parts of an animal or plant decompose before the layers build up enough to make a fossil.

Some replacement fossils show dinosaur bones.

Replacement fossils are often made from hard parts such as bones, shells, and teeth. They are three-dimensional (3-D). This means there are indents or bumps. People can feel the details.

Molds and casts are made during replacement fossilization. First, any soft parts decompose. Second, the hard parts leave an **impression** in the mud or sand surrounding the remains. This is the mold. A shell may push against sediment. The sediment eventually hardens into a rock. It shows details of the outside of the shell. Grooves of the shell can be felt and seen in this part of the fossil.

impression—a mark, line, or indent made on the surface of an object

TRACE FOSSILS

Trace fossils show animal activity. Footprints are a type of trace fossil. Paleontologists study them to learn about how animals walked. Poop is also a trace fossil. Paleontologists can learn about what animals ate from their poop. Tyrannosaurus rex poop fossils show they ate all of their food, including the bones.

Third, water flows through the rock. It removes the minerals originally in the hard parts. At the same time, minerals such as opal or calcium fill the mold. This is the cast. The cast shows details of the inside. It can show lines where muscles or organs were.

The most well-known way to make a fossil is **permineralization**. Permineralization happens to the hard parts of animal and plant remains.

permineralization—a type of fossilization that involves minerals and being buried in the ground

The remains are buried in sediment. Layers pile on top. Water flows through the animal or plant. Minerals in the water get left behind in the very small spaces in the tissues of the plant or animal. The minerals take the shape of the remains.

The cast part of a fossil rises up out of the rock, while the mold part forms an indent in the rock.

As pressure builds, the minerals harden into rock. The rock shows the details of the remains. The fossil is 3-D. Many dinosaur bones are fossilized this way. This is how petrified wood forms.

Many impressive dinosaur skeletons fossilized by permineralization.

In a lab, permineralization happened in about two months. It likely takes much longer in natural conditions.

Most fossils are made by being buried in sediment. However, fossils can be made in other ways. Some animals are completely frozen in ice. The ice freezes the whole plant or

animal. It preserves the soft and hard parts. Insects can be preserved in **amber**. Amber fossils are rare and valuable. The entire insect is preserved. Paleontologists can study ice and amber fossils in detail.

amber—a hard, dark yellow material made from thick, sticky liquid that comes out of trees and hardens

CHAPTER FOUR

DISCOVERY

Fossils may form deep in the earth. But they don't stay there. The earth changes a little every year. Water levels rise and lower. Pieces of land move farther apart. Movement can expose fossils. Slowly, over many years, layers from the bottom move to the top. They get pushed up by other layers.

Erosion uncovers fossils too. Erosion is a slow process. It is when rocks are worn down. Wind and water cause erosion. They change the size or shape of a rock.

FACT

From the 1870s to the 1890s, two American paleontologists competed to see who could find more fossils in the West. They found more than 100 new species.

The rock gets smaller or smoother. It might break into pieces. Many fossils appear because of erosion. The layers on top of them are worn away.

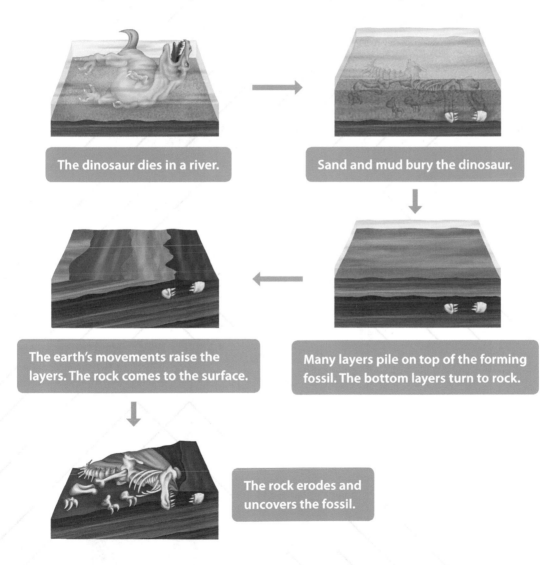

The dinosaur dies in a river.

Sand and mud bury the dinosaur.

The earth's movements raise the layers. The rock comes to the surface.

Many layers pile on top of the forming fossil. The bottom layers turn to rock.

The rock erodes and uncovers the fossil.

It takes a lot of time and careful work to dig up fossils.

Fossils help scientists learn about the history of life on Earth. Paleontologists study fossils. They learn about what animals and plants lived in the past. They study bones of animals to see how they walked. They study plants to see how they grew.

ANCIENT FOSSILS

Dinosaur fossils are still being discovered today. In 2018 a dinosaur fossil was found in China. It was 127 million years old.

They look at animals and plants to see what the **climate** used to be like in the past. From fossils, paleontologists have discovered that Antarctica, which is covered in snow year-round, once had tropical plants and animals. Geologists can use information about the animal and plant impressions to study rocks. Rocks tell them about the earth and how it has changed.

The youngest fossils can be 10,000 years old. Others are thousands or millions of years old. Fossils reveal what the world was like many years ago.

climate—the temperature, weather, and environment of a certain area

GLOSSARY

amber (AM-bur)—a hard, dark yellow hard material made from thick, sticky liquid that comes out of trees and hardens

climate (KLYE-mit)—the temperature, weather, and environment of a certain area

decompose (dee-kum-POZE)—to break down into smaller pieces

fossilization (fah-sul-i-ZAY-shun)—the process of dead animal or plant remains turning into rocks

geologist (jee-AH-luh-jist)—a person who studies rocks and is an expert on them

gravity (GRAV-i-tee)—a force that pulls objects with mass together; gravity pulls objects down toward the center of Earth

impression (im-PRESH-uhn)—a mark, line, or indent made on the surface of an object

mineral (MIN-ur-uhl)—a material found in nature that is not an animal or plant

oxygen (AHK-si-juhn)—a gas that is used for many things on Earth, including breathing and breaking things down

paleontologist (pay-lee-uhn-TAH-luh-jist)—a person who studies fossils and is an expert on them

permineralization (pur-min-ur-uhl-i-ZAY-shuhn)—a type of fossilization that involves minerals and being buried in the ground

remains (ri-MAYNZ)—the dead body of an animal or plant

scientist (SYE-uhn-tist)—a person who uses observation and experiments to study the natural world

sediment (SED-uh-munt)—material such as small grains of sand, rock, or earth matter that are moved by wind or water before they settle

ADDITIONAL RESOURCES

FURTHER READING

Holtz, Thomas R., Jr. *Digging for Triceratops: A Discovery Timeline.* Dinosaur Discovery Timelines. North Mankato, Minn.: Capstone Press, 2015.

Oxlade, Chris. *Fossils.* Rock On! Chicago: Heinemann Raintree, 2016.

Sawyer, Ava. *Fossils.* Rocks. North Mankato, Minn.: Capstone Press, 2019.

Taylor, Paul D. *Fossil.* DK Eyewitness Books. New York: DK, 2017.

CRITICAL THINKING QUESTIONS

1. Geologists and paleontologists can learn about Earth millions of years ago by studying fossils. Why do you think it's important to learn about the past?

2. Fossils can be made in different ways. Choose any animal or plant. Think about its environment and describe the process of how it could become a fossil. Use evidence from the text to support your answer.

3. Scientists guess that many plants and animals do not become fossils after they die. What is one reason a fossil may not be made?

INTERNET SITES

DK Find Out! Fossil Hunters
https://www.dkfindout.com/us/dinosaurs-and-prehistoric-life/fossils/fossil-hunters/

DK Find Out! Fossils
https://www.dkfindout.com/us/dinosaurs-and-prehistoric-life/fossils/

Science Kids: Fossil Facts
http://www.sciencekids.co.nz/sciencefacts/earth/fossils.html

INDEX

ABOUT THE AUTHOR

Emily Hudd is a full-time children's author who loves writing nonfiction on a variety of topics. She lives in Minnesota with her husband.